Lord, I Forgive Myself

Dr. Tommy Beeker

ISBN 979-8-88751-772-8 (paperback)
ISBN 979-8-88751-773-5 (digital)

Christian Faith Publishing
832 Park Avenue
Meadville, PA 16335
www.christianfaithpublishing.com

Printed in the United States of America

Acknowledgments

First and foremost, I want to thank my Lord and Savior Jesus for His unconditional love and forgiveness, along with the gifts He has given me that I desire to use to bring Him glory. Thank you, Lord, for all you have and are doing in my life. May this book bring you great praise and worship.

Secondly, I want to honor my wife, Jackie, who has been a great strength in my life and a strong encourager who reminds me to pray and seek the Lord in all I do. Thank you, my precious Bebe, for loving me and being such a blessing in my life. You are my forever-soon!

And finally, I want to thank all those fellow Christians who have stood with me as I have written this book. Because of your support, this work has been published and has gotten into the hands of so many that need to find peace of mind in the absolute forgiveness of God and the joy of forgiving themselves.

I need to sit here a minute and really think things over. Today's sermon really troubled me. It overwhelmed me, and frankly, I was very upset. I wish, in some ways, I hadn't gone to church this morning.

First of all, every time I go, I feel like a hypocrite, ashamed and quite alone. I go because I know that it's supposed to help me in my relationship with Jesus and other Christians. However, I also go because I feel guilty if I don't show up.

On top of that, I struggle so hard getting up on Sunday morning and driving myself to church to be around Christians that really seem to be genuinely happy and full of the joy of the Lord. Me, I just feel embarrassed, so I put on a happy face hoping no one knows how I really feel. I sit quietly in the back row so no one will approach me and realize the sadness I feel in the depths of my heart and soul.

As I sit in my pew each Sunday morning, I observe the other people worshiping with such joy on their faces. I truly wish I could feel that kind of joy and peace, but I don't! Instead, I feel ashamed and so deeply unworthy of being in the presence of such powerful and God-loving people. Then when the presence of the Lord is evident as His Spirit fills the church, I really want to run and hide because I don't feel worthy of such wonderful peace that fills the sanctuary.

Reflecting again on the sermon today, the pastor's topic was "The Power of Forgiveness." For years, I have heard about how God forgives those who confess their sins and repent. There is a verse I remember hearing in 1 John 1:9 that says, *"If we confess our sins, he is faithful and just to forgive us our sins, and to cleanse us from all unrighteousness."*

I know the Bible says that. And I want to believe it, and I guess I sort of do. But I can't help hating myself for having made such a mess out of my life. I have confessed my sins to Jesus hundreds of times. Yet over and over, I find myself doing the same sins with no victory over them. Do I really mean it when I go to Jesus to seek His forgiveness? After all, I keep on sinning. Do I ask for His forgiveness the wrong way? Do I ask for His forgiveness just to get over the guilty feelings? Is there any hope for this lost soul, this sinner, this unworthy human being, this poor excuse for a Christian?

I am reminded that forgiving yourself was one of the things the pastor talked about this morning. Yeah right! How can I forgive myself when I am not even sure Jesus has or is willing to forgive me? If I were Jesus, I wouldn't even consider forgiving me, especially because I just keep doing the same things over and over.

I understand forgiving others, and I find it easy to forgive others because they seem worthy of my forgiveness. Me, I am not worthy, and I am a poor excuse for a person who is supposed to be a Christian! Frankly, being honest with myself, I am, at least in my mind, an embarrassment to the Body of Christ. If the people in my church really knew what kind of a sinner I am, they would probably ask me to leave the church. Frankly, I wouldn't blame them.

My brothers and sisters in Jesus at my church have no idea how I struggle with certain sins in my life and how much I fail daily in keeping His commandments. I see them in church so happy and free in Jesus, and it makes me feel sad, so isolated, and unworthy to even be in their presence. I can really relate to Paul in the Bible when he says in Romans 7:24, "*O wretched man that I am! Who shall deliver me from this body of this death?"* That's me, a wretched Christian. Indeed, who shall deliver me from this body of death?

I remember the pastor saying at the end of his sermon today that each of us needs to spend time alone with Jesus and have a heart-to-heart talk about our lives, our sins, and our hopes of living a life worthy of the gospel of Christ. Even considering talking with Jesus makes me want to hide from His presence. Yet this sermon today, as I said before, really troubled and overwhelmed me.

I was and still am very emotional about all this. I know in my heart that I, a Christian, hurt the heart of Jesus every time I sin. It's like I am driving those nails into His precious hands and feet over and over every time I sin! That is one of the reasons I cannot forgive myself. Oh, Jesus, why do You love me? Do You really love me or just put up with me? Why did You die on the cross for me? I am such a miserable excuse for a Christian, Lord. Jesus, why would You even want to sit down face-to-face with me and talk to me alone?

Child, because I love you!

Lord, is that really You? Or am I just imagining that I hear Your voice?

Yes, My child. I am here, and how I desire to spend time with you. Just you and Me! I have really missed talking to you! We used to talk a lot when you first got saved. But recently, you have been very quiet and very withdrawn from others, especially Me.

Jesus, I can really feel Your presence! This cannot be real! Yet I feel safe and well, even at peace. However, Lord, I also feel so unclean, ashamed, and so unworthy to have this time with You alone, Lord!

Child, I would not be here if I didn't love you unconditionally. I want you to feel My love when I am close to you. I don't want you to feel ashamed or unworthy. You are absolutely so precious to Me!

Jesus, why do I feel Your presence especially now?

Because, My precious child, your heart's desire is to know and understand how much you are loved by Me, yet you question My love for you almost every day. Still, you also desire to feel the peace and joy you see in others. So I am here today because I want you to fully understand and feel My love for you, My precious one.

Jesus, I have so many sins in my life that make me feel very ashamed. Why are You even taking the time to talk to this miserable excuse for a Christian? You know how much I sin. How can You even love me knowing what kind of a sinner I am?

Because, My precious one, I love you unconditionally! Do you know what *unconditionally* means?

Not really. I have never felt unconditional love from anyone, ever!

My dear precious child, when I love one of Mine—and you, child, are indeed one of Mine—I love with no limits of any kind. My Word says in Romans 5:8, "*But God commendeth his love toward us, in that, while we were yet sinners, Christ died for us.*"

Commendeth, My child, means to make one acceptable. You see, My precious child, My Father and I made you acceptable through Me the day you accepted Me as your Savior.

Let Me teach you something important. The *th* at the end of the word, My child, simply means an ongoing process. Therefore, We commendeth or continually make you acceptable in Our eyes and in Our hearts, no matter what.

No matter what, Jesus?

No matter what, My precious child!

Child, My Word says in 2 Corinthians 5:21, "*For he hath made him to be sin for us, who knew no sin; that we might be made the righteousness of God in him.*"

My precious one, I never knew sin, committed sin, nor could I because I am now and was God in the flesh when I came to earth. Yet being God in the flesh, I came to earth for this very reason. I came to die on that cross and become the sins of all mankind. I didn't take on the sins of the world—I became the sins of the world. That is why I cried out on the cross, "My God, my God, why hast thou forsaken me."

You see, My child, for the first time in My eternal existence, I was separated from My Father because God, who is holy, cannot look upon sin. Through Me becoming the sins of mankind and shedding My blood for every man, woman, and child, My Father makes all who believe and accept Me as their personal Lord and Savior the very righteousness of Himself. This includes you! When you accepted Me as your Savior, My Father made you totally righteous in His sight forever! That is why you are accepted or commended and always loved and totally forgiven.

Child, let Me ask you this. How righteous is God?

Well, of course, He is totally righteous, Lord.

That's right! Remember, I became the sins of all mankind, and that includes yours. When a person accepts My sacrifice on the cross and receives Me as their Savior, My Father makes them the very righteousness that He is in and of Himself. When you accepted Me as your Savior, My child, you became the very righteousness of God.

Lord, how can I be righteous, let alone the righteousness of God? I am a sinner. Sinners are not righteous. As a matter of fact, the Bible says in Romans 3:10, *"As it is written, There is none righteous, no, not one!"* So how can I be righteous in any way, shape, or form? It just doesn't make any sense, Lord!

Child, you are right. Humans are sinners, and they are not righteous in and of themselves. The Bible even says in Isaiah 64:6, *"But we are all as an unclean thing, and all our righteousnesses are as filthy rags; and we all do fade as a leaf; and our iniquities, like the wind, have taken us away."*

Man has no righteousness in and of himself, My child. That is why, My precious one, My Father's plan of the ages was to make a way for His greatest creation, mankind, which includes you, to become righteous so you and all of mankind could be in the presence of the true and Holy God. His plan was for Me to become the sins of every human from Adam to the last person born on Earth. He did this so that each human who willingly accepts Me as their Savior and Lord would become righteous in His sight. How He views His creation is what is really true, not what man thinks or says about others or what a person says or thinks about themselves.

Why, Lord? Why would God the Father, being all-knowing, have You—His Son—even take the time to die for mankind, let alone for a sinner like me? You know every sin I have committed, struggled with yet today, and will probably commit tomorrow. Why, Lord? How can You love someone who is so unfaithful and sinful as me, Lord?

Child, many times have you heard the words in John 3:16, *"For God so loved the world, that he gave his only begotten Son, that whosoever believeth in him should not perish, but have everlasting life."*

My Father and I are indeed all-knowing, as you stated. However, because We are all-knowing, We also knew the condition of man in his sinful state even before the fall of

Adam and Eve in the garden of Eden. Yet We so loved the world. The word *world* here, My precious one, means all of mankind. We knew that mankind in and of themselves could never realize and obtain a state of being sinless or righteous. Therefore, the eternal plan of My Father was to give mankind a chance to obtain righteousness through believing in Me and My sacrifice for mankind. Through believing and accepting Me, each person would receive not only total and absolute forgiveness but would also receive everlasting life. This, My precious one, means you too!

Really? Me, a sinful and unworthy Christian?

Child, let Me put it this way. God so loved you that He gave His only begotten Son—Me; that if you believe in Me, you will not perish but will instead have everlasting life! When you accepted Me as your Lord and Savior, you started believing and trusting Me. Therefore, My Father totally forgave you, canceled all your debts forever, and has given you everlasting life so you can have a personal relationship with the Father and with Me.

Child, there is another verse that is often overlooked and rarely shared from the pulpit of so many churches. It is found in John 3:17. Let's read it together. *"For God sent not his Son into the world to condemn the world; but that the world through him might be saved."*

Child, I did not come to Earth to condemn the world but to save the world through My sacrifice. I did not come to condemn you either. I came to save you!

In fact, My child, Romans 8:1 says, *"There is therefore now no condemnation to them which are in Christ Jesus, who walk not after the flesh, but after the Spirit."*

There is no condemnation of Christians. None! This includes you, My child! You are in Me, and I am in you. With Me and the Holy Spirit living in you and your body being the temple of the Holy Spirit, there is no way you can be condemned for your sins because you walk now in the Spirit. Before you were saved, you walked in the flesh of sinfulness. But when you were *born again,* you no longer walked in the flesh of sinfulness but are now walking in the Spirit of righteousness!

Jesus, being a human with a fleshly body, how can I not walk in the flesh? I really don't understand what You are teaching me.

Let Me explain a little bit more about not walking in the flesh. Let's read together Romans 8:8–9: *"So then they that are in the flesh cannot please God. <u>But ye are not in the flesh, but in the Spirit, if so be that the Spirit of God dwell in you.</u> Now if any man have not the Spirit of Christ, he is none of his"* (emphasis mine).

When you were *born again*, My precious child, the Holy Spirit and I took residence in you because your body became the temple of the Holy Spirit. The Spirit of God now dwells in you. Therefore, you are no longer walking in the flesh. When you were lost in your sins, you could not please God. But now that you are *born again*, you walk daily in the Spirit of God, and God is well pleased with you. Again, My precious one, the Spirit of God dwells in you!

Let's look at 1 Corinthians 6:19–20: *"What? know ye not that your body is the temple of the Holy Ghost which is in you, which ye have of God, and ye are not your own? For ye are bought with a price: therefore, glorify God in your body, and in your spirit, which are God's."*

Jesus, are You telling me that my body is holy?

Yes, that is exactly what I am telling you. Let Me ask you this. Since I am God in the flesh and the Holy Spirit is God, would God, who is holy, live in an unholy place?

No, Lord, You and the Holy Spirit would never live and be in an unholy place, ever!

That's right! When you were *born again*, your body became holy so that the Holy Spirit and I could come and live in you and be with you always, no matter where you are in this world or what is going on in your life. As a matter of fact, your body became sanctified, glorified, and set apart to become a temple that We could dwell in and be close to you always.

Oh my goodness, Lord. That is amazing! However, Lord, it is so hard for me to comprehend the love of God. Maybe, Lord, I don't fully understand the heart of my heavenly Father. Could that possibly be, Jesus?

Yes, child, you and millions of Christians around the world don't fully understanding the heart of My Father, nor My heart toward each of you. As a matter of fact, My Word says in Micah 7:18–19:

> *Who is a God like unto thee, that pardoneth iniquity, and passeth by the transgression of the remnant of his heritage? He retaineth not his anger forever, because he delighteth in mercy. He will turn again, he will have compassion upon us; he will subdue our iniquities; and thou wilt cast all their sins into the depth of the sea.*

Child, when your heavenly Father forgives, it is total and absolute forgiveness! He pardons all your sins, removes the need for you to pay for your sins, and He doesn't stay angry forever because, child, your heavenly Father delights in giving you mercy instead! He has compassion for you because He knows your human weakness. Then He helps you to become less sinful, and He also casts all your sins into the depths of the sea. Remember in 1 John 1:9, it says, "*If we confess our sins, he is faithful and just to forgive us our sins, and to cleanse us from all unrighteousness.*"

When you pray and ask for forgiveness, I not only forgive you, but I also help you to become less sinful and cleanse you from all unrighteousness, which is a process as you grow in the faith and the grace of My Father.

Child, let's look at Micah 7:19: "*He will turn again, he will have compassion upon us; He will subdue our iniquities; And thou wilt cast all their sins into the depths of the sea.*" My precious child, the word *subdue* means to restrain, meaning that I help you to say no to your sins and the temptations that come your way as a human. Now, My child, let's read together Psalm 103:12: "*As far as the east is from the west so far hath he removed our transgressions from us.*"

Not only does your heavenly Father cast your sins into the depths of the sea, but He also removes your transgressions, your sins, as far as the east is to the west, which is beyond measure.

This is almost too much to grasp, Lord! Jesus, I feel like I should pay for my own sins because You are holy and I am not. Besides, You know how much I struggle. That is one of the reasons I cannot forgive myself, as the pastor talked about today in church. Forgiving myself, Lord, seems wrong because I know in my heart how much I sin every day. In my mind, I don't deserve to be forgiven. So why would I even consider forgiving myself? This is so hard, Jesus, to understand!

Child, I heard you say this before I came to talk with you, "That is one of the reasons I cannot forgive myself." We need to deal with these *reasons* you cannot forgive yourself. But for now, let's set that aside and come back and talk more about that later.

Okay, Lord.

Let's read again John 3:17: "*For God sent not his Son into the world to condemn the world; but that the world through him might be saved.*" Again, let Me put it this way. For God sent Me into the world not to condemn you, but so you, My child, through Me might be saved, forgiven, and made totally righteous in the sight of God, your heavenly Father. By accepting Me as your Savior, My Father gave you the right to call Him Father, even Abba Father, meaning "Daddy!" Do you understand?

I am beginning to, Lord. But You and I know how much I sin. Why would You ever want to continue to be my Savior and have me as Your child and the Father to have me as one of His children?

Child, do you remember the story in My Word about the prodigal son?

Yes, I remember reading and hearing it in church.

Let's take a look at a portion of the story in Luke 15:11–24, and let Me ask you a few questions.

Okay.

And he said, A certain man had two sons: And the younger of them said to his father; Father, give me the portion of goods that falleth to me. And he divided unto them his living. And not many days after the younger son gathered all together, and took his journey into a far country, and there wasted his substance with riotous living. And when he had spent all, there arose a mighty famine in that land; and he began to be in want. And he went and joined himself to a citizen of that country; and he sent him into his fields to feed swine. And he would fain have filled his belly with the husks that the swine did eat: and no man gave unto him. And when he came to himself, he said, How many hired servants of my father's have bread enough and to spare, and I perish with hunger! I will arise and go to my father, and will say unto him, Father, I have sinned against heaven, and before thee, And am no more worthy to be called thy son: make me as one of thy hired servants. And he arose, and came to his father. But when he was yet a great way off, his father saw him, and had compassion, and ran, and fell on his neck, and kissed him. And the son said unto him, Father, I have sinned against heaven, and in thy sight, and am no more worthy to be called thy son. But the father said to his servants, Bring forth the best robe, and put it on him; and put a ring on his hand, and shoes on his feet: And bring hither the fatted calf, and kill it; and let us eat, and be merry: For this my son was dead, and is alive again; he was lost, and is found. And they began to be merry.

Now child, let Me ask you a few questions. Even though the son, upon leaving his father, sinned by taking his portion of the goods and wasting his substance with riotous living, at what point during this time when he was not in close fellowship with his father did he stop being the son?

Hmmm…well, looking at it, he didn't.

That's right! The prodigal son never stopped being the son! He remained the son even while he was away from his father and living in sin. Now let Me ask you this. After the son saw the errors of his ways and decided to go back home to his father and repent and become willing to just be a servant, what was the father's reaction as the son returned home?

Hm? Show me please. Show me, Jesus.

Let's look closely at verse 20: "*And he arose, and came to his father. But when he was yet a great way off, his father saw him, and had compassion, and ran, and fell on his neck, and kissed him.*" Child, what was the father's reaction?

When his father saw his son a great way off, the father had compassion and ran and fell on his neck and kissed him.

That's right! Before the son even got all the way home, the father was out there looking for him; and when he saw him a great way off, the father did not wait until the son arrived and repented. Instead, the father, immediately seeing him coming home, had compassion and ran to his son. And notice, My dear child, the father did not condemn the son, nor did he punish him. Instead, the father fell on his neck and kissed him, welcoming him back with total acceptance, and then he celebrated his homecoming.

Why, Lord?

Because, My precious one, that is the love of a father. That is the love of your heavenly Father. When you leave His and My presence through your sins, you never stop being a son, a child of God, nor could you ever stop being a son of God. You never stop being loved and wanted.

When you leave Our fellowship through your sins, you are only losing the closeness you desire and see in others. Again, you never stopped being a son of God, and you never stopped being Our precious child. I am always watching for you to come home, and when I see you coming back through your prayers of repentance, I don't wait for you to even finish. I am already on My way to hug you and welcome you back with no con-demnation whatsoever! Also you need to know that the phrase *son of God* is neither male nor female. The term *son of God* in reference to humans is their new position with My heavenly Father once they are *born again*. It simply means you are a child of God regardless of you being male or female.

Wow, Lord! This truth from Your Word is, well, overwhelming, and yet I still feel so unworthy of such love and compassion.

My dear child, there is another scripture I want us to look at, and I believe it will help you even more to understand the heart of your heavenly Father. Let's look at 2 Peter 3:9: "*The Lord is not slack concerning his promise, as some men count slackness; <u>but is longsuffering to us-ward, not willing that any should perish, but that all should come to repentance</u>*" (emphasis mine).

Your heavenly Father keeps His promises and is not willing that any human should die without the opportunity to come to repentance and establish a new and eternal relationship with Him. It is, however, the choice of every human to accept the Father's plan of salvation or to reject it. The Father has given mankind the gift of *free will* to accept or reject His love and His forgiveness through Me, His Son.

Remember, child, I said in My Word, in John 14:6, "*I am the way, the truth, and the life: no man cometh unto the Father, but by me.*" No one, no human being can become righteous, forgiven, and then have the right to eternal life without accepting the free gift of salvation from God through Me and My sacrifice on the cross. However, child, you accepted my sacrifice for yourself, and therefore, the Father has given you eternal life with no strings attached!

Jesus, this is overwhelming and yet amazing to hear! Maybe that's why it is called amazing grace!

Very true, My precious one. Let's now look at another verse that I know will help you understand even more. Let's look at Ephesians 2:8–9: "*For by grace are ye saved through faith; and that not of yourselves: <u>it is the gift of God</u>: Not of works, lest any man should boast*" (emphasis mine) Your salvation, My child, is a gift! You don't earn a gift. If you had to earn a gift, it would no longer be a gift, would it?

No, Lord, it would not be a gift. A gift is free.

That's right. Salvation is a gift from My Father to all and any who repents and asks for forgiveness of their sins and asks Me to be their Lord and Savior. No one can ever earn it or lose the free gift of eternal life.

Jesus, I just didn't know all that applied to me personally. Yet, Jesus, I feel so ashamed when I do pray and repent, and I am also not always sure if You hear me or forgive me.

Child, let Me show you another scripture about your heavenly Father's heart concerning forgiving you. It is found in Jeremiah 31:34, where it says that God will not only forgive the sins of Israel, but He will remember them no more.

> *And they shall teach no more every man his neighbor, and every man his brother, saying, Know the Lord: for they shall all know me, from the least of them unto the greatest of them, saith the Lord: <u>for I will forgive their iniquity, and I will remember their sin no more.</u> (Emphasis mine)*

Jesus, my heavenly Father will not remember my sins?

That's right, My child. So let's look at another verse that will help you understand more. Let's read Psalm 103:10–11: *"He hath not dealt with us after our sins; Nor rewarded us according to our iniquities. For as the heaven is high above the earth, So great is his mercy toward them that fear him."*

My precious child, this means God forgets your sins because He has totally forgiven you. Your heavenly Father chooses not to bring up your sins to Himself or others or throw them in your face. When your sins come racing back into your mind, you have two choices. You can choose to dwell upon them, thus resulting in guilty feelings, or you can choose to fill your mind with thoughts of the awesome God who has and always will totally forgive you. That is why you should always thank and praise Him for His unconditional love and forgiveness.

I do thank Him, Lord, yet I really struggle so hard, Jesus, with dwelling on my past sins and the ones I am trying not to do now. I get so depressed and sad because I know I am hurting Your heart, Jesus! Because I struggle so hard with dwelling on my past sins and the ones I struggle with now, it is hard for me to hold on to God's unconditional forgiveness. I feel like I am in a spiritual battle.

You are in a spiritual battle! However, it's your dwelling on your past and your focus on the current sins in your life that are causing you to feel so unworthy.

Child, you have an enemy whose name is Satan, who hates you and doesn't want you to be free from your past. He wants you to stay focused on your past so you will not be free to experience the total love and forgiveness of your heavenly Father. And, My precious child, it's you dwelling on the past that gets you into depression. You have what some call *stinkin' thinkin'*.

Also, you need to block out those lies of the devil and believe My Word, not the words of a liar like Satan. My words are truth, and his words are lies! As a matter of fact, he is the father of lies.

Child, focus on My Word and believe My Word, not the lies of Satan, nor the lies you believe about yourself, nor the false teachings of so many Christian denominations. My Word is the final authority, not what you think is true or what you may have been taught by some false teaching from the church. My Word, the Bible, is the absolute final authority of all truth. My Word is the truth! Here is what I prayed one day to My heavenly Father about all of you in John 17:17: "*Sanctify them through thy truth; thy word is truth.*"

Child, the Bible also says in Philippians 4:8, "*Finally, brethren, whatsoever things are true, whatsoever things are honest, whatsoever things are lovely, whatsoever things are of good report; if there be any virtue, and if there be any praise, think on these things.*"

Child, what is true is that you are saved, forgiven, sanctified, justified, and filled with the Holy Spirit. What is honest or sincere is you are unconditionally loved by Me and your heavenly Father. What is lovely is the joy of your Father's heart as He looks upon you. He doesn't see a sinner. He sees a forgiven, sanctified, and justified saint! What is of a good report is that you are born again and washed clean of all your sins through my shed blood. What is virtue, or of great value, is that you are a child of the living God!

With all that in mind, you should not be wasting time beating yourself up and listening to the lies of Satan. Instead, you should, when struggling with the lies of Satan, be praising Me and your heavenly Father for loving you more than you even love yourself! Child, when you are dwelling on the past and your current sins, you are rejecting the love of your heavenly Father and, in some ways, saying, "Lord, I reject Your unconditional love." Do you really mean to do that in your heart?

No, Jesus! No way! I don't mean to reject Your forgiveness. I just feel so unworthy.

Child, you are unworthy in and of yourself. But as I told you before, you are worthy through Me! My love for you doesn't depend on you feeling unworthy, nor does it depend on you being *sinless*. Your worthiness is based on what I have done for you on the cross! Period! You accepting My sacrifice on that cross has made you worthy in the eyes of My Father and in My eyes too.

Okay, Jesus, I am beginning to see what You are saying. However, Lord, when I pray, Lord, and come to repent, do You really hear my prayers?

I hear all your prayers, even those silent ones you pray when you are in pain and emotionally hurting.

I feel like You should condemn me for my sins, not forgive me.

Your feelings have nothing to do with My unconditional love for you. Your feelings often lie to you. Too often, My children follow their feelings instead of the truth of My Word! It breaks My heart as I see My children making decisions based on their feelings instead of what is the truth of My Word.

I do verbally punish myself, Jesus, and I have made a lot of decisions based on my feelings instead of believing Your Word. But I have a question that has bothered me a lot, Lord. And maybe this question will help You understand why I struggle so much with accepting Your forgiveness and forgiving myself.

Okay, child. What is your question?

Lord, I have heard some pastors say that if we sin, we will lose our salvation. Is this true, Jesus? Can I lose my salvation because I sin?

Let's go back to John 3:16 and look at a couple of words in particular: *"For God so loved the world, that he gave his only begotten Son, that whosoever believeth in him should not perish, but have everlasting life."*

Look at the last two words, *everlasting life*. The word *everlasting* means "without end, constant, and eternal." Once you are saved, you have everlasting life, period! You cannot lose it. Just like the prodigal son, who never lost this relationship as a son of his father, you can never lose your relationship with Me or your heavenly Father. Remember, My child, We talked about this earlier in Our conversation. You are eternally saved!

But, Jesus, I often hear I can lose my salvation by sinning, by not going to church, by not keeping a bunch of rules set by the church leaders, and by not reading my Bible enough. I am, at times, Jesus, very scared of losing my salvation. I have even heard that you can lose your salvation by blaspheming the Holy Spirit. This frightens me, Jesus! It really does!

Child, My precious child, let Me ask you this. Can you imagine My Father coming to Me and saying, "Son, I am sorry, but this child of Yours has sinned one too many times. I know You paid a high price for their sins, but the blood that You shed on that cross just wasn't enough to cover all these sins. I am sorry, but those sins outweigh the precious blood You shed on the cross for this lost child. I am going to take their salvation away." Can you imagine My Father saying this to Me?

No! Never, Lord, would Your Father say that to You? However, Jesus, what about this question? What about backsliding? Doesn't that mean I have lost my salvation? And, Lord, what about blasphemy of the Holy Spirit?

No, My child. You have not lost your salvation. Let Me talk to you about backsliding first, and then I will talk to you about blasphemy of the Holy Spirit.

Backsliding simply means you have left the closeness and intimacy of Me and My Father. *Backsliding*, My child, means to fall back into wrongdoing or a bad habit after an attempt to live a sinless life. My precious child, every Christian backslides every day! There is not one Christian—regardless of their position in the church—that doesn't, in some way, shape, or form, backslide because they all still sin every day in sinful thoughts, words, or deeds.

Remember, there are none righteous. No, not one. Your position in the church doesn't make you better than someone else, for all have sinned and fallen short of the glory of God. A Christian's righteousness is found only in their relationship with Me. No works can save you or keep you saved. You are saved because of what I have done for you on the cross. Period! Again, let's turn to Ephesians 2:8–9: "*For by grace are ye saved through faith; and that not of yourselves: it is a gift of God: not of works lest any man should boast.*"

Child, you are saved through faith, which is a gift of God. You are not saved by works, lest any man should boast in and of himself as being worthy of salvation. God gave you the faith so you could be saved through

Me. God is not going to share His glory with anyone. Your salvation is a gift that comes through the faith God gave you. Since all have fallen short of the glory of God, no one can be saved by not sinning, by going to church, or by following a bunch of man-made rules. No human can even keep the Ten Commandments, let alone some man-made rules that supposedly get you saved or keep your salvation secure.

My precious child, every human and every Christian is always in a backslidden condition. The human condition, since the fall of man in the garden of Eden, has never changed. Humans are born into sin. They are sinners by nature. No one has to teach a child to sin. It happens automatically because all humans are sinners at birth.

When Adam and Eve ate from the tree of the knowledge of good and evil, they understood—for the first time—the knowledge of good and evil, which has been passed down to all mankind ever since. That is why My Father and I made a way for man to have peace with God through My death on the cross. Every Christian backslides every day. You, My precious child, are not alone, nor are you unique.

Okay, Lord, I understand that so far. But again, what about the blasphemy of the Holy Spirit?

This, child, is another false teaching in the church today. Christians cannot blaspheme the Holy Spirit. Let's go to My Word and look closely at what My Word says, not what preachers are preaching, which only puts people back into bondage. Let's look at chapter 3 of the Gospel of Mark.

I was in the city called Capernaum, speaking at the temple and ministering to the sick, healing them, and casting out unclean spirits. However, the scribes—who had come down from Jerusalem—started accusing Me of doing all this with the power of Beelzebub and by the prince of devils.

Now let Me teach you something before I go on. Beelzebub is one of the seven princes of hell. He is the chief lieutenant of Lucifer, and he presides over the order of the flies. The name Beelzebub means "lord of the flies." The prince of devils is another demon that is over all devils or demons.

Now let's look at the following Bible verses:

And the scribes which came down from Jerusalem said, He hath Beelzebub, and by the prince of the devils casteth he out devils. And he called them unto him, and said unto them in parables, How can Satan cast out Satan? And if a kingdom be divided against itself, that kingdom cannot stand. And if a house be divided against itself, that house cannot stand. And if Satan rise up against himself, and be divided, he cannot stand, but hath an end. No man can enter into a strong man's house, and spoil his goods, except he will first bind the strong man; and then he will spoil his house. Verily I say unto you, All sins shall be forgiven unto the sons of men, and blasphemies wherewith soever they shall blaspheme: But he that shall blaspheme against the Holy Ghost hath never forgiveness, but is in danger of eternal damnation. Because they said, He hath an unclean spirit.

(Mark 3:22–30)

Now, child, let Me show you this. The scribes were making the accusation that I was ministering with the power of Beelzebub and the prince of devils. So I told them, "*How can Satan cast out Satan? And if a kingdom be divided against itself, that kingdom cannot stand. And if a house be divided against itself, that house cannot stand. And if Satan rise up against himself, and be divided, he cannot stand, but hath an end.*"

The thing they did not understand was that I was ministering with the power of the Holy Spirit because I was God in the flesh and came in the power of the Holy Spirit to bring God's love to mankind.

However, they—the scribes—said I was ministering with the power of Satan, which is blaspheming the Holy Spirit. You see, it was the scribes that blasphemed the Holy Spirit because they were operating in the flesh and did not recognize who I was. They blasphemed the Holy Spirit. A Christian, My dear child, cannot blaspheme the Holy Spirit.

Why, Lord?

Because the Holy Spirit dwells in every Christian, the same Holy Spirit that is in Me and was in Me when I was on Earth.

Look again at verse 29–30: *"But he that shall blaspheme against the Holy Ghost hath never forgiveness, but is in danger of eternal damnation. Because they said, He hath an unclean spirit."* See what it says, in verse 30: *"Because they said, He hath an unclean spirit."* Would a Christian ever say I was ministering in the power of Beelzebub or the prince of devils? Would a Christian say I had an unclean spirit?

No, Lord. I know I would never say that about You.

So you see, My child, a Christian cannot commit this unforgivable sin. But a person sold out to Satan could, and many have committed this unforgivable sin. But Christians cannot because the Holy Spirit dwells in their bodies because a Christian's body is the temple of the Holy Spirit. And since the Holy Spirit is God, He would never dwell in an unholy place. And since I am God in the flesh, and the Holy Spirit and the Father and I are one, I could never have ministered in the power of Satan. Does this help you understand?

Yes, Lord, I am so happy You explained that. The point I see here is that we, Christians, need to believe what the Bible says and teaches, not the teachings of a particular denomination. If I hear You right, Lord, the Bible is the final authority, not a church denomination.

Yes, that's exactly right, My precious child.

Lord, since all humans are sinners, what hope is there?

Child, I am that hope. Again, I am the way, the truth, and the life. Man cannot, nor will he ever be able to save himself from his fallen condition. The only hope man has is to see and accept that he is a sinner in need of a savior. My Father and I know this, and yet We have made a way for all mankind, every human, male or female, to find forgiveness and to be reconciled to My Father.

Lord, what do You mean *reconciled*? What does that mean?

The word *reconciled* simply means to restore to a friendship or to have peace with someone you have offended. No matter how hard a person tries, no one can reconcile themselves with God. Only God can reconcile a person and restore a relationship with Him. That reconciliation only comes through accepting Me as Savior and Lord and the sacrifice I made for mankind.

Is that in the Bible, Lord?

Yes. It is found in several places. But for now, let's look at Romans 5:10: *"For if, when we were enemies, we were reconciled to God by the death of his Son, much more, being reconciled, we shall be saved by his life."*

Through My death on the cross, man can be reconciled (restored) in a relationship with God. However, reconciliation only comes when there is true repentance and acceptance of My sacrificial death on the cross. Then and only then can man receive atonement for their sins.

Lord, what do You mean *atonement*?

In many ways, child, *atonement* is the same thing as *reconciliation*. In Romans 5:11, it says, "*And not only so, but we also joy in God through our Lord Jesus Christ, by whom we have now received the atonement.*"

With My death on the cross and your accepting that sacrificial death on your behalf, My Father honored My sacrificial death, and My death then atoned for all your sins—all of them: the past, present, and future. Notice it says at the end of this verse the words, *the atonement.*

<u>There is only one atonement,</u> child, and it only happened once! It happened for you when you prayed, confessed your sins, and asked for My forgiveness. At that moment, My Father and I totally forgive you, child, for all the sins you have ever done, are doing, and will do in the future, because they are atoned for and paid for in full!

Child, read with Me now from 1 Peter 3:18: "*For Christ also hath once suffered for sins, the just for the unjust, that He might bring us to God, being put to death in the flesh, but quickened by the Spirit."*

When I died on that cross, and I being the only just (holy) one, I died for the unjust and all of sinful humankind so that I could bring all of mankind to My Father. I only died once, and it was at that one death, child, that I atoned for the sins of the world and paid the price for all your sins and the sins of the whole world. This, My precious one, means I paid the price for all your sins and reconciled you to God forever.

When you accepted Me as your Savior and Lord and repented your sins, the death I suffered on the cross paid for all your sins, and you were reconciled. Your sins were atoned for through My death. You will never have to pay for your sins. I paid that price for you because, My child, I loved you even then while I was dying on the cross. Do you understand that today, in My very presence, your sins are atoned for? You have received the atonement and have been through My death reconciled to your heavenly Father forever!

Oh, my precious Jesus. What You have just shown me in the Bible is beginning to help me understand Your amazing grace, forgiveness, and unconditional love.

Child, My Father wishes that all should be saved, and none should perish. Here, again, is a verse from the Bible that shows My Father's heart. Look again at 2 Peter 3:9: *"The Lord is not slack concerning his promise, as some men count slackness; but is longsuffering to us-ward, not willing that any should perish, but that all should come to repentance."* My Father and I are patient with mankind, and We are not willing that any should perish but that all should come to repentance.

Child, Our heart's desire is that you understand that all your sins are paid for and that you have not only been reconciled but you have also been justified, glorified, filled with the Holy Spirit, and are the temple of the Holy Spirit. When you accepted Me as your Lord and Savior, your body became the temple of the Holy Spirit, as we read before in 1 Corinthians 6:19, *"What? Know ye not that your body is the temple of the Holy Ghost which is in you, which ye have of God, and ye are not your own?"*

Upon accepting My sacrificial death on your behalf, your body, child, became the temple of the Holy Spirit, and He and I dwell in you and with you forever. That is how precious you are to Us!

Dear Jesus, my heart is filled with such joy! I am so glad You came to talk with me today. I needed to hear these things. Maybe I have heard them before, but today these truths have become more real to me.

Child, the forgiveness of the Father is forever! He has not only forgiven you, but He sees you as a saint, a holy person, righteous, perfect, and acceptable. And He sees not your sins but your heart toward Me, His only begotten Son, whom you have loved and accepted as your Savior. You have filled His heart with such joy, My child, knowing that you loved Him enough to accept His offering of atonement and reconciliation through His Son, Me, Jesus!

So if I hear You right, Jesus, I cannot be, nor ever will be condemned for sinning.

That right, child. Let's look at Roman 8:1–4:

> *There is therefore now no condemnation to them that are in Christ Jesus, who walk not after the flesh, but after the Spirit. For the law of the Spirit of life in Christ Jesus hath made me free from the law of sin and death. For what the law could not do, in that it was weak through the flesh, God sending his own Son in the likeness of sinful flesh,*

and for sin, <u>condemned sin in the flesh</u>:That the righteousness of the law might be fulfilled in us, who walk not after the flesh, but after the Spirit. (Emphasis mine)

Therefore, My precious one, there is no condemnation for you right now, at this very moment, and forever because you are in Me, Jesus Christ. You once walked in the flesh before you became saved. Now that you are born again, your body is the very temple of the Holy Spirit where He and I dwell in you and with you.

You see, My child, the law—the Ten Commandments—which no man can keep, cannot ever save a person even if they try to keep the law. The sin of mankind has made the law weak, and no one can save themselves or do enough good works to be saved. You have been freed from the law of sin and death. And what is the law of sin and death? Read this in Romans 6:23: *"For the wages of sin is death; but the gift of God is eternal life through Jesus Christ our Lord."*

Child, when I came into the world to pay the price for sin, I did not come to condemn man <u>but to condemn sin</u>! Do you understand?

You did not come to condemn me, Jesus, but to save me. I got it!

Okay, My child, let's look at Romans 8:3: *"For what the law could not do, in that it was weak through the flesh, God, sending His own Son in the likeness of sinful flesh, and for sin, <u>condemned sin</u> in the flesh"* (emphasis mine).

Do you understand? There is, therefore, now, right now, in the very moment of time no condemnation for you, My precious child. The wages of your sin were paid for by Me on that cross at Calvary. And when you accepted My Father's gift of eternal life, you were free from the law of sin and death! Once and for all, forever! I did not come to condemn mankind but to condemn sin in My own flesh on that cross. I defeated and fulfilled the law of sin and death.

Jesus, these truths from Your Word have made me feel free again. Even though I sin daily, as all mankind does, if we are Your children, then there is now no condemnation for us. Right?

That right, child. No condemnation. Just love, forgiveness, and the joy of having you as one of My Father's children. The problem is that, for whatever the reason, you have been condemning yourself, and frankly, you have no right to. Why? Because My death set you free from any condemnation.

Child, let's look again at John 3:17: *"For God sent not his Son into the world to condemn the world; but that the world through him might be saved."*

I was sent into the world not to condemn the world but to save the world. I came to the earth not to condemn you but to save you. There is no condemnation because I paid the price.

Child, do you remember earlier in our conversation when I told you that you are justified, glorified, and filled with the Holy Spirit?

Yes, I remember You saying that.

Do you know what *being justified* means?

No, not really, Lord.

There are a lot of verses in the Bible concerning being justified. Let's start with Romans 8:30: *"Moreover whom he did predestinate, them he also called: and whom he called, them he also justified: and whom he justified, them he also glorified."*

Child, with all that you struggle with, not being able to forgive yourself and fully receiving the forgiveness of your heavenly Father, you need to understand this very important part of your salvation. You are not only saved and forgiven, you are also justified. Do you know what it means to be justified?

No, Lord, I have no idea.

Justified is a legal term that signifies acquittal, which means found not guilty of a crime or, in this case, of sin. Oh, My dear child, if only every Christian fully understood what being justified means! In the sight of My Father, through My sacrificial death on the cross, a person accepting My death to pay for their sins, My Father finds them *not guilty*!

My precious one, when you received Me as your Lord and Savior, My Father acquitted you from all your sins and has found you *not guilty*!

Wow, Lord!

Here, My child, is another verse from my Word. It is found in Romans 5:1–2: *"Therefore being justified by faith, we have peace with God through our Lord Jesus Christ: By whom also we have access by faith into this grace wherein we stand, and rejoice in hope of the glory of God."*

As you see in My Word, Christians are justified (found not guilty) through faith. Therefore, Christians have peace with God through Me. And Christians have access by faith to God's amazing grace where they stand (abide) every day. That is why Christians can rejoice in the hope of the glory of God. So, My precious one, you too are justified (found not guilty) through the faith you have in Me and My sacrificial death on the cross. And remember this too, faith is a gift from God. You could not believe in the Father and Me if He had not given you the faith in the first place! Faith is a gift!

Okay, Lord, but what about doing good works?

Let's look at Romans 3:28: *"Therefore we conclude that a man is justified by faith without the deeds of the law."* Child, since you—as a Christian—are justified by faith, without the deeds of the law, which no one can keep, your justification is not based on doing good works or keeping a heavy load of rules often pressed upon Christians by some Christian denominations. Your justification comes through the faith God gave you as a gift.

Faith is a gift from the Lord?

Yes, let's look again at Ephesians 2:8–9: *"For by grace <u>are ye saved through faith</u>; and that not of yourselves: <u>it is a gift of God</u>: Not of works, lest any man should boast"* (emphasis mine).

Look carefully at this verse, My child. It is by grace that you are saved through faith, and faith is not something you have in and of yourself. Faith is a gift from God. My Father, as I said before, is not going to share His glory with any man. Salvation comes through faith and not by works. My Father gives all of mankind the gift of faith so they can be saved. Faith is a gift from God.

Where does faith come from, Lord?

In My Word, in Romans 10:17, it says, "*So then faith cometh by hearing, and hearing by the word of God.*" When you started hearing My Word through the Bible, faith started coming to you by hearing the Word of God. The more you are in the Word—reading and studying My Word—your faith grows, and you begin to gain the knowledge and joy of knowing the full grace and mercy of your heavenly Father. That is why I say in 2 Timothy 2:15, "*Study to show thyself approved unto God, a workman that needeth not to be ashamed, rightly dividing the word of truth.*"

This is so powerful and freeing, Lord.

Now, My child, let's look at something else We talked about before, and that is the word *glorified*. Referring back to Romans 8:29–30, We read,

> *For whom he did foreknow, he also did predestinate to be conformed to the image of his Son, that he might be the firstborn among many brethren. Moreover whom he did predestinate, them he also called: and whom he called, them he also justified: and whom he justified, them he also glorified.* (Emphasis mine)

Being gloried, My child, in this verse means that you are being conformed to the image of God's Son. You are being conformed, even transformed to be holy, sanctified, and predestined to be Christ-like. Your heavenly Father has predestinated you to be conformed into My image.

Now, child, We need to talk about you.

What do You mean, Lord?

For years, you have been condemning yourself for your sins and punishing yourself for being a sinner. While it is true in this lifetime that you and all of mankind are sinners, you, My child, are a born-again sinner saved by grace, not by works. Let's look again at Ephesians 2:8–9: *"For by grace are ye saved through faith, and that not of yourselves: it is the gift of God: Not of works, lest any man should boast."*

Your salvation was not accomplished by your works, by you being perfect and never sinning. Your salvation came as a gift from God. Nor does your works or the lack of them take away your salvation. Salvation is the gift of God. You cannot earn your salvation, My child, nor can you lose your salvation because of your lack of works or lack of sinning. The gift of salvation is just that—a gift!

Now there is one more thing about works I want you to understand. Sadly, the verse I am about to show you has been used by denominations to teach that one can lose their salvation. But you now know that you cannot lose your salvation. With that said, let's look at James 2:26: *"For as the body without the spirit is dead, so faith without works is dead also."*

Lord, what does that mean?

As you know now, My child, works do not save a person. Neither do works justify nor make one righteous before My Father, nor are works a means to salvation. The works that Christians do are the fruit of the Spirit that grows in that person who is obedient to God's commands and transformed by His grace. Christians are saved not by works or deeds, but by the amazing grace of God, redeemed by My work on the cross.

My child, let's together read Titus 3:5–6: "*Not by works of righteousness which we have done, but according to his mercy he saved us, by the washing of regeneration, and renewing of the Holy Ghost: That being justified by his grace, we should be made heirs according to the hope of eternal life*" (emphasis mine).

Child, it is not by works of righteousness that a person is saved. They are saved by the grace of My Father alone.

Look with Me now at Romans 4:4–5: "*Now to him that worketh is the reward not reckoned of grace, but of debt. But to him that worketh not, but believeth on him that justifieth the ungodly, his faith is counted for righteousness*" (emphasis mine).

Child, your faith is what My Father and I count for your righteousness. When you decided to believe in Me, the one that justifieth the ungodly, your faith in Me was counted as righteousness because your righteousness is found only in Me, My child. However, if a person is doing works so they can get saved or keep their salvation, their reward—if you will—is of debt, not of grace.

Jesus, that makes a lot of sense. Thank You for showing me that in Your Word. But also, Lord, I know that I have sinned a lot in my life, and I know I have not forgiven myself for my sins. Yet today, You have shown me that I cannot save myself, and I cannot lose my salvation, which is the gift of God. Yet, Lord, while I am really beginning to understand my salvation and that through You, I am eternally saved, I don't know how to forgive myself for some of the awful things I have done in my lifetime.

Help me, Jesus. I want to be free from this condemnation I feel and the guilt I feel every time I fail You and sin in Your sight. I am like the prodigal son. I know I have done wrong and have sinned before You and do not deserve to be loved by You. Yet You do love me, and You love me unconditionally! Lord, how do I love myself and forgive myself as You love me and have forgiven me?

First of all, My child, you have been believing a lie from the devil himself. He does not want you to be at peace with your salvation. He hates you and hates that you are now a child of the living God. He wants to destroy you and rob you of the joy of knowing and appreciating your salvation through Me. You have been lied to by both Satan and from the false teaching that often comes from Christian denominations who do not teach the whole truth of My Word. They instead have, like the Pharisees, added their own laws and rules in order to either control people and teach them damnable heresies while wanting to be looked up to as the final authority, when indeed My Word is the final authority.

The Bible tells us, child, in 1 Timothy 4:1–5:

> *Now the Spirit speaketh expressly, that in the latter times some shall depart from the faith giving heed to seducing spirits, and the doctrines of devils; Speaking lies in hypocrisy; having their conscience seared with a hot iron; Forbidding to marry, and commanding to abstain from meats which God hath created to be received with thanksgiving of them which believe and know the truth.*

The Bible also states in 2 Timothy 4:3–4, "*For the time will come when they will not endure sound doctrine; but after their own lusts shall they heap to themselves teachers, having itching ears; And they shall turn away their ears from the truth, and shall be turned unto fables."*

What happens in many "Christian" denominations is that they deny the truth of God's Word and change it so it is more suitable to their own interpretation of My Word. Yet My Word says in 2 Peter 1:20–21, *"Knowing this first, that no prophecy of the scripture is of any private interpretation. For the prophecy came not in old time by the will of man, but holy men of God spake as they were moved by the Holy Ghost."*

Sadly, My child, many "Christian" denominations have come up with their own private interpretations of My Word through the development of corrupt Bible versions which remove the truth and add corruption and false teachings so that the body of Christ has become perverted with false teachings, especially about salvation. My Word also says this in 2 Peter 2:1–2, *"But there were false prophets also among the people, even as there shall be false teachers among you, who privily shall bring in damnable heresies, even denying the Lord that bought them, and bring upon themselves swift destruction"* (emphasis mine).

Lord, it is at times confusing when I read my Bible and see that what I am reading doesn't line up with what I am being taught from the pulpit or from preachers I hear on TV or the radio. But I have just figured that they know better than I do because they are pastors, teachers, and evangelists.

Child, part of the problem is that you have become dependent on the teachings from maybe your pastor or preachers on TV or the radio. There is a point where you have to take some responsibility too. My Word says in 2 Timothy 2:15, "*Study to show thyself approved unto God, a workman that needeth not to be ashamed, rightly dividing the word of truth.*"

While it is true that a lot of false teachings are coming from the church today, you have a responsibility to study the Word of God for yourself. As you have seen today, the Bible is the *only truth*. It is, in fact, the *final authority.* And today, My child, you have seen that you are totally and absolutely forgiven by God and free from any condemnation. Now the time has come for you to let go of the lies you have either been taught or believed and hold fast to the truth of My Word.

Okay, Lord, what do I do now?

It is time you let go of the lies that you are not worthy of My love and forgiveness. My Word today has shown you the truth, and My truth will and has set you free to let go of the lies that you are not worthy in the sight of My Father.

Help me, Lord! Help me to let go and forgive myself and hold on to the truth Your Word has shown me today. I want so much to have the joy You want me to have in You.

Child, if I have forgiven you, if My Father has forgiven you, then who are you not to forgive yourself? In not forgiving yourself, you are denying the truth of My Word, which has clearly shown you that you are loved, forgiven, sanctified, glorified, and filled with My Holy Spirit and that you are indeed a child of the living God.

I am so sorry for believing the lies, Lord. Today, I choose to no longer believe the lies, and I fully accept Your Word as the final authority concerning my relationship with You and my heavenly Father.

Child, I forgive you!

Thank You, Jesus! And I receive Your forgiveness!

Good, My child. Now let's pray together. Repeat after Me, My child!

Heavenly Father, in the precious name of Jesus and through the truth of Your Word, I, today, am deciding to accept the truth of Your Word and believe in my heart that I am totally and absolutely forgiven of all my sins, even the ones I struggle with today. In the name of Jesus, my Lord and Savior, I stand up against the lies of my enemy, Satan, and reject his attacks and bind up those attacks through the precious blood of Jesus.

Today, Lord, I choose to believe Your Word over and above those thoughts that enter my mind and cause me to doubt the truth concerning my salvation. Today, I choose to be free from the bondage of my past sins, my current sins, and the ones I will commit tomorrow because I know and believe God's Word over and above those thoughts that condemn me. Thank You, Lord, for Your total and absolute forgiveness found through the blood of Jesus. I am, today, free from all condemnation and stand firm in the grace and mercy of my Lord and precious Savior, Jesus Christ. Amen

That was very good, My child.

Thank You, Lord. Jesus?

Yes, My precious child!

I want to pray my own prayer now.

Okay, My child. I am listening.

Dear Jesus, I come before You humbly today, asking You to help me forgive myself. I have looked back on my past for way too long. I am tired of feeling like I could have done better every single day. To be honest, Lord, a part of me knows that it is true. I really could have made better choices. But I cannot go back and change the past. With Your help, Jesus, the only thing I can attempt to control is my future. I cannot live life backward. Lord, right now, I release all my anxiety into Your hands. It is not Your will that I hate myself for all the things that I have done. Lord, when I hate myself, I hate the very thing that You have created and restored through the blood of Jesus. I know that this, too, is a sin and hurts Your heart. I don't want to hurt Your heart, Jesus, or reject Your forgiveness anymore. Therefore, with Your help today, Lord, I fully accept Your unconditional forgiveness, knowing this blesses You and touches Your heart. In Jesus's name. Amen!

Jesus?

Yes, My child?

Lord, I forgive myself.

About the Author

Dr. Tommy Beeker holds a doctorate in theology along with two master's in theology and education and three bachelor's degrees in theology, education, and counseling. He is also an ordained pastor of forty years.

Dr. Beeker is the author of *The Truth About The TRUTH*. Even though he is retired from the pulpit, he still ministers to the body of Christ through an online weekly Bible study entitled Bible Believers' Fellowship found on Zoom and is writing books to reach out to Christians around the world.

Lord, I Forgive Myself is the second book he has written with the hope of helping millions of Christians who struggle with forgiving themselves. It is his heart's desire that as you read this book, you will find the joy of knowing and understanding the complete forgiveness of your heavenly Father and being able to say to Jesus with confidence, "Lord, I forgive myself."

To contact the author write to LordIForgive Myself@gmail.com

9 7 9 8 8 8 7 5 1 7 7 2 8